Basic
CANDLE MAKING

0 11557 02476 0

Basic
CANDLE MAKING

All the Skills and Tools You Need to Get Started

Eric Ebeling, *editor*

Scott Ham,
candle maker and consultant

Photographs by
Alan Wycheck

STACKPOLE
BOOKS

Published by
STACKPOLE BOOKS
5067 Ritter Road
Mechanicsburg, PA 17055
www.stackpolebooks.com

Printed in China

10 9 8 7 6 5 4 3

First edition

Photographs by Alan Wycheck
Cover design by Tracy Patterson

Library of Congress Cataloging-in-Publication Data

Basic candle making / Eric Ebeling, editor.— 1st ed.
       p. cm.
    Includes bibliographical references.
    ISBN 0-8117-2476-X
    1. Candlemaking. I. Ebeling, Eric.

TT896.5 .B375 2002
745.593'32—dc21

                                                          2002021229

ISBN 978-0-8117-2476-0

Contents

Acknowledgments

So many people helped to transform this book from concept to reality, and I apologize to anyone I have failed to recognize here.

My gratitude to: Alan Wycheck of Wycheck Photography in Harrisburg, Pennsylvania, whose skills behind the lens captured the vision of this book; Scott Ham of the Gettysburg Candle Company and Moonacre Ironworks, whose expertise drips like melted wax from these pages; Beth, David, and Kenny Fine, for the use of their once-spotless kitchen as a candle making workshop/photography studio; Kellie Carpenter, for supplying me with all of that prime candle making equipment; Kay and Devron Wilcox, for serving as a courier service; Bill Stevens, also known as the Candle Man, for taking time to demonstrate; Amy Wagner, for all the help; Ron Zappile, for the gracious use of his scenic backyard as a shooting locale; and last, but far from least, my wife Andrea and son Alec, who never complained as odd smells wafted through the house and strange creations cooled on the countertops. Thanks for your patience, you two; I guess you know what we'll be giving as gifts this year.

—Eric Ebeling

1

Candle Making Materials and Equipment

For the beginner, the two most important ingredients needed for candle making can't be found in any craft store. They are time and patience, and properly used, they will serve you well.

The basic projects in this book require no highly advanced skills to complete. They were selected because they represent the basic building blocks of all candle making. Once comfortable with the skills and concepts of each project, you will be ready to create a nearly limitless number of candle variations and modifications on your own—whether its experimenting with colors and aromas, making custom molds, or dreaming up your own kind of unique candle.

Getting to that point, however, requires a patient, measured approach. Think of yourself as a chef, turning plain wax into an attractive main dish using color dyes and fragrances as spices. Like in cooking, preparation and execution in candle making are best not rushed. Make sure you have the recommended amount of time needed to complete each project. If you don't, wait until you do.

Take some time to learn about the materials and equipment needed for successful candle making. Some of the items listed on the following pages are probably in your kitchen cupboards right now. Other more specialized pieces of equipment need to be purchased in a craft or department store, or online.

Each project requires a different combination of the items listed. For that reason, a detailed checklist for the container, molded, dipped, and rolled beeswax candle projects is included at the start of each chapter. It can be copied and taken along to the store like a shopping list. It's a good idea to know the function and price range of each item on your list before you enter the store.

All amounts listed are in U.S. standard measurements. Consult the measurement conversion chart on page 104 for metric equivalents.

A word of advice learned the hard way: Wax can be stubborn to remove completely from pots, pans, and accessories, so don't use the good cookware or utensils when making candles.

MATERIALS

WAX

Paraffin, a petroleum by-product, is the recommended wax for making the hot-wax candle projects in this book. Odorless, colorless, and relatively inexpensive, quality paraffin is available in most craft supply stores, where it is sold mainly in 10-pound slabs or 1-pound bags of pellets.

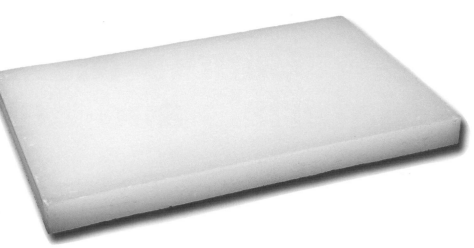

Different formulations of paraffin melt at different temperatures, from about 100 degrees Fahrenheit (30 degrees Celsius) to 160 degrees Fahrenheit (71 degrees Celsius). Beginners should choose an easy-to-use paraffin with a melting point of about 140 degrees F. (60 degrees C.), which won't turn to liquid too quickly or require too much heat to melt properly. Expect to pay $1 to $2 per pound. Pellets made of beeswax, which needs no additional dyes or fragrances, can be melted and used in the same way as paraffin.

Keep in mind that a hammer and chisel (or screwdriver) are needed to break away chunks of paraffin from a slab prior to melting.

The shelves of the local craft store teem with all manner of specialty waxes, each of which serves a distinct purpose outside the scope of the projects set forth here. They include dip and carve wax, a soft, malleable substance that is softer than most waxes and can be shaped without breaking; gel wax, which has a consistency of set gelatin and requires no heat to use in containers; and wax blends with special characteristics, such as low or high melting points, greater hardness, and limited shrinkage during cooling. Consider exploring these alternatives after gaining experience with the basic ingredients.

STEARIN

This additive allows the candle to hold more color and makes the paraffin harder. Known also as stearic acid, this fat derivative makes paraffin more opaque, helps dyes and scents mix well with melted paraffin, and reduces drips while burning. Once made exclusively from animal fat, stearin is now also made from plant oil, such as palm. Solid at room temperature, it is used in a roughly 10 to 1 ratio with wax, so for 16 ounces of wax, 3 tablespoons (1.5 ounces) of stearin are needed. Expect to pay up to $10 for a 1-pound bag of soap-like flakes or pellets; available in most craft stores.

While stearin is the recommended paraffin additive for container, molded, and dipped candles, a number of other additives are available in craft stores. Most of them, such as a trademarked substance called Vybar and a category of additives known as microwaxes, are also designed to harden candles, allow them to burn longer, and make them hold color better. Some supply companies make paraffin mixtures that already contain additives and need no further embellishment. Advice: Read labels carefully when purchasing.

WICK

Wick size must be matched to suit the diameter of the candle for proper burning. A wick that is too small will quickly drown in a pool of melted wax. A wick that is too large will smoke, sputter, and burn too hot. Manufacturers use a labeling system that specifies correct wick/candle combinations, so keep that in mind while shopping.

Most regular-size candles, those up to 3 inches in diameter, require just one central wick for proper burning. Very large candles may require two or more evenly spaced wicks.

Cotton Core (Round)

Cotton Core (Flat)

The two main types of wick are cotton core and wire core. Cotton core wick, which is usually made up of strands "braided" around a thick cotton center, is recommended for making poured, dipped, and beeswax candles. It can be either round or flat braid.

Wire core wick is recommended for use in container candles, which burn the longest of all candles. As the name indicates, a thin piece of wire—usually made of zinc—runs through the center of the wick, giving it more support and allowing it to burn for a greater duration than standard wick. Avoid using older wire core wick, because it may contain lead, a standard core ingredient in manufacturing a number of years ago. Its use has been discontinued because of health concerns.

Wire Core

Commercial wicks are relatively inexpensive and very reliable, so homemade wicks made of paper or twine are not recommended. Expect to pay about $3 for 20 feet of wick; available in most craft stores.

4

METAL WICK TAB

This device grips the wick, helps anchor it, and keeps it straight in a container candle during wax pouring and cooling. Expect to pay about $2 for a package of 24; available in most craft stores.

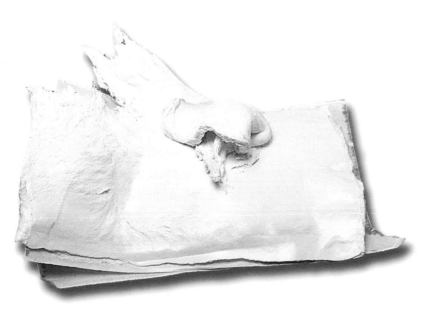

MOLD SEALER

This sticky gum-like substance plugs the wick hole at the bottom of a candle mold to prevent wax from leaking. It also is used to hold the wick tab in place inside the container while hot wax is poured. Expect to pay about $3 for a 1-ounce package; available in most craft stores. Cost-saving tip: String caulk, available in most hardware stores, works fine as an inexpensive substitute for mold sealer.

DYE

Commercial candle dyes are concentrated, so a small amount will produce strong, deep colors across the color spectrum. Dye is sold in hard squares or chips. Usually $^1/_8$ to $^1/_4$ ounce of dye is enough to color 1 pound of paraffin. Because dye formulas vary from manufacturer to manufacturer, package directions should be followed.

Custom colors can be made by mixing dyes much like artists do on their palettes. For instance, adding yellow and blue dyes to wax will create a shade of green. Making a specific custom color is an exercise in trial and error.

Expect to pay about $3 for a $^1/_2$-ounce package of dye; available in most craft stores.

Homemade dyes or other colorings not specifically designed for candle making should be avoided, because igniting them could prove to be unsafe, or they could clog the wick and prevent it from burning properly. For this same reason, crayons should not be used.

Mixing Primary Colors

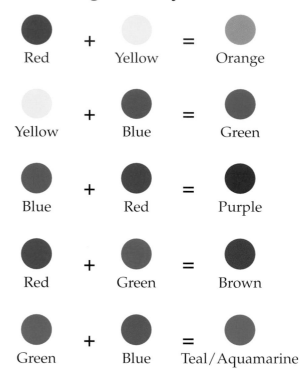

Red + Yellow = Orange

Yellow + Blue = Green

Blue + Red = Purple

Red + Green = Brown

Green + Blue = Teal/Aquamarine

Note: Different shades of these colors can be achieved by the amounts you mix into your wax.

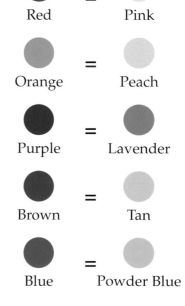

Red = Pink

Orange = Peach

Purple = Lavender

Brown = Tan

Blue = Powder Blue

FRAGRANCE OIL OR SCENT DISKS

Like color dyes, fragrance oils and scents are potent—a little goes a long way. Oils are formulated to combine well with melted wax and give off a strong aroma when burned; scent disks come in solid form, much like dye disks, and are generally not as aromatic.

For most commercial scent preparations, $^1/_8$ to $^1/_4$ ounce of oil or $^1/_4$ to $^1/_2$ ounce of solid is adequate for 1 pound of wax. Commonly produced scents include lavender, lilac, honeysuckle, rose, gardenia, jasmine, hyacinth, blueberry, banana, orange, grapefruit, cherry, apple, peach, strawberry, mulberry, coconut, tangerine, bayberry, sandalwood, pine, patchouli, mint, coffee, chocolate, vanilla, cinnamon, and clove. Scents can be combined to create unique results. Expect to pay about $4 for a 2-ounce bottle or 1-ounce package; available in most craft stores.

Beginners should not add household herbs, spices, or extracts to candles because they may pose a fire risk or prevent proper burning. Some essential oils, strong extracts from aromatic flowers, plants, and trees, can be used successfully in candle making; others will not work because of their formulations. Novices should avoid using them and stick with scents specifically designed for candle making.

Custom Mixing Fragrances

Any fragrance formulated for candle making will produce a good result by itself. Experienced candle makers often like to take their creations one step further by mixing fragrances—usually oils—to produce custom scents. It's an inexact science governed by trial and error. Some fragrances are naturally stronger than others, and intensity can vary from manufacturer to manufacturer.

Once you get comfortable making candles with single, basic scents, let your creativity—and your nose—be your guide. Keep a notebook handy to jot down notes about combinations and amounts so you will know how to recreate those aromas that turned out well. Below is a chart showing just some of the combinations possible when mixing fragrances.

Apple	+	Cinnamon and Vanilla	=	Apple Crisp
Rose	+	Vanilla	=	Baby Powder
Strawberry	+	Maple Sugar	=	Strawberry Pancakes
Apple	+	Caramel	=	Caramel Apple
Vanilla	+	Cherry	=	Cherry Cheesecake
Lemon	+	Vanilla	=	Lemon Custard
Orange	+	Clove	=	Autumn Spice
Honeydew Melon	+	Cucumber	=	Cucumber Melon
Orange	+	Peach	=	Fuzzy Navel
Coffee	+	Hazelnut and Vanilla	=	Hazelnut Coffee
Coffee	+	Chocolate	=	Mocha
Lemon	+	Strawberry	=	Strawberry Lemonade
Vanilla	+	Cinnamon	=	Crumb Dessert
Chocolate	+	Cherry	=	Baked Alaska
Peppermint	+	Strawberry	=	Candy Cane

BEESWAX SHEETS

Made of pressed and formed beeswax, these textured, rectangular sheets are typically sold in packages of two, each about 8 inches wide and 18 inches long. The sheets are slightly sticky and pliable, and they are ready for rolling straight from the package.

No dye or fragrance needs to be added, because the sheets are already colored for use.

Candle wick is often included in the package; check the contents to be sure. Expect to pay up to $10 for a complete kit; available in most craft stores.

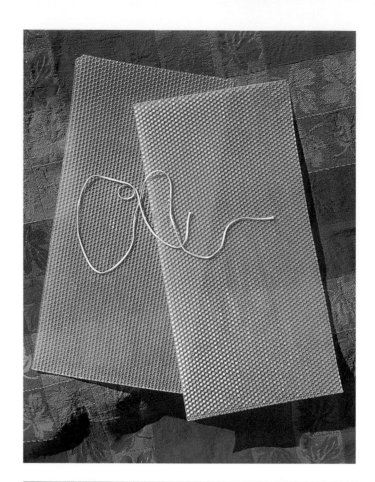

CANDLE WAX REMOVER

This dissolves hardened wax and makes it easier to clean the work area and equipment. Expect to pay about $10 for a 5-ounce bottle; available in craft supply stores. Cost-saving tip: Any concentrated, citrus-based cleaning fluid will remove wax. This type of cleaner is available in most grocery stores.

CONTAINERS

Glass canning or jelly jars are perfect for candle making because they are designed to withstand high temperatures without cracking. Metal containers and ceramic mugs may be used also, as long as they can withstand direct flame and heat.

Many craft stores stock a variety of plain and adorned glass jars for candle projects. Expect to pay about $10 for a box of a dozen canning jars; available in most grocery, department, and craft supply stores.

CANDLE MOLDS

These are typically made of hard plastic, metal, aluminum, or rubber and come in a number of shapes and sizes.

A sturdy plastic pillar mold—easy to handle, easy to clean—that holds a pound of wax is recommended for the projects detailed in this book. Other plastic molds can be used to make candles in geometric shapes, such as rectangles, squares, and pyramids. Expect to pay up to $25 for a hard plastic mold; available in most craft supply stores.

Metal and aluminum molds are sturdy and reliable as well. They can be used to produce a wide range of candle shapes, including pentagons, stars, cones, and cylinders. Metal molds often must be warmed before they are filled, because cool metal can cause hot wax to harden too quickly. This can create air bubbles, frosting, and other surface mistakes on the candle.

Rubber or flexible molds made of latex are somewhat trickier to use than hard plastic or metal molds, because they are more delicate and require careful handling to avoid tearing.

Many novelty and floating candles shaped like fruits, flower blossoms, figurines, and a host of other decorative objects are produced using rubber molds. Stearin should not be used in these molds because it may react with the rubber and dissolve it. Vybar or a similar additive should be used instead.

Soft plastic molds, which resemble gelatin dessert molds, are available for making a variety of unusual and detailed candles. In addition, two-piece molds that are clamped together can be used to make spheres and similar shapes. They often are tricky to use, and beginners should consider using them only after they have gained some experience.

HEAT SOURCE

An electric or gas stove is ideal for heating candle wax to the appropriate temperature.

An electric hot plate, available in most department or kitchen supply stores, will work fine as well. Expect to pay about $25 for a hot plate.

DOUBLE BOILER

Used to heat paraffin, a 2-quart capacity model made of stainless steel or aluminum is recommended to allow for easier cleanup. Expect to pay about $30; available in most department or kitchen supply stores.

You also can create an improvised double boiler by placing a small saucepan inside a larger one. Since wax is very difficult to remove completely from pans, consider using old pots and pans for candle making purposes.

THERMOMETER

A candy or cooking thermometer with a range between 100 and 356 degrees F. (38 and 180 degrees C.) is recommended for monitoring molten wax temperatures. Expect to pay about $20; available in most kitchen supply, department, and craft stores.

KITCHEN SCALE

Needed to weigh proper quantities of paraffin. Expect to pay about $10 for a general-use model; available in most department or kitchen supply stores.

METAL POURING JUG

This jug is used to pour hot wax into containers and molds, and it is a good container for holding melted wax during candle dipping.

Because pouring must be done slowly and without splashing, a jug manufactured with a formed spout is recommended. Choose a model that holds a half gallon of liquid. Expect to pay about $10; available at most department or kitchen supply stores.

DIPPING CAN

This specialized piece of equipment is used to make longer-than-average dipped candles. The depth of the can requires dozens of pounds of wax to fill it to capacity. The model shown stands more than 2 feet high. Expect to pay $50 or more, depending on the size; available from candle making suppliers.

SCISSORS OR CRAFT KNIFE
Either will work fine for cutting wick to proper length and trimming it after the candle has cooled. A craft knife is needed for cutting beeswax sheets prior to rolling.

APRON
Protects clothing from errant wax drips and spills.

OVEN MITTS
Any mitts designed for kitchen use will work well for handling hot pots, molds, and containers during and after the pouring of molten wax.

SPOON
Choose a spoon with a handle about 12 inches long, so dyes and fragrance oils can be stirred into the wax safely.

WOODEN ICE CREAM STICKS
These serve two purposes in candle making. The stick holds the wick to keep it from falling into the mold or container during hot wax pouring. It also is used to poke holes in the surface of the cooling wax to release trapped air. Expect to pay $1 for a pack of two dozen sticks; available in most grocery or craft stores.

WOODEN OR PLASTIC RACK

A clothes-drying rack made of slender wooden or plastic bars is perfect for hanging pairs of taper candles to dry after dipping.

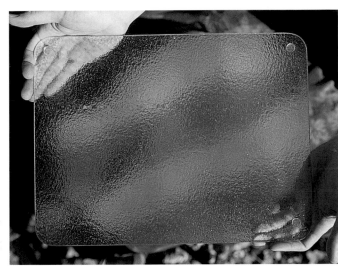

CUTTING BOARD OR PLACE MAT

This provides a smooth, untextured surface for rolling beeswax candles. A glass or plastic surface is recommended.

MEASURING SPOONS

A ring of metal or plastic measuring spoons containing standard measures (teaspoons/tablespoons) is recommended for adding stearin and fragrances to the hot wax.

RULER OR STRAIGHT-EDGE

Used as a guide when cutting sheets of beeswax.

HAIR DRYER

Used to heat cool beeswax sheets to make them more supple and easier to roll.

15

NEWSPAPERS
Old newsprint will save your countertops and other parts of your work area from wax drips and spills. Save enough papers to cover work area surfaces to a thickness of three or four sheets.

PAPER TOWELS, CLEANING RAG
Keep some on hand for quick cleanup of drips and spills and for cleaning equipment at the end of the project.

WAX PAPER
The non-stick properties of wax paper are needed when rolling freshly dipped candles to smooth them out. The paper also can be used to cover work surfaces when making rolled beeswax candles; a smooth cutting board or laminated place mat works well for beeswax candles as well.

EMPTY COFFEE CAN
Used to hold leftover wax for future projects.

SMALL PLASTIC BAGS
The type used for sandwiches is perfect for storing candle supplies such as dyes and wick material.

NYLON STOCKING
Imperfections on the surface of a candle can be buffed out using a piece of nylon from pantyhose. Use an old piece, because wax is difficult to remove from material.

If you have difficulty locating materials or equipment, you can find them easily on the Internet. Just log on to your favorite search engine and type "candle making" + "supplies" to contact hundreds of online retailers.

Candle making enthusiasts often scour flea markets and swap meets for inexpensive pots, pans, and other items that can be used for projects.

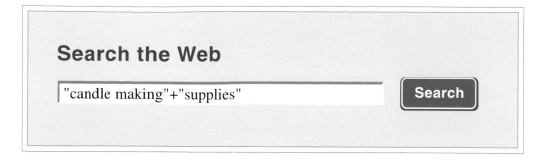

Search the Web

"candle making"+"supplies"   **Search**

2

A Good Work Environment

The average kitchen provides the proper workspace for making container, molded, and dipped candles, provided that a heat source is within easy reach of the area where hot wax will be poured.

For the rolled beeswax project, which does not involve melting wax, any sturdy, flat surface will do.

Clear away small appliances, utensil holders, and other items from countertops near the work area. Despite care and caution during candle making, some hot wax always seems to find its way onto nearby surfaces not covered with newspaper. A little effort spent moving these small items now will save time when it comes to cleanup later.

Countertop space must be large enough to accommodate all materials and equipment except for the double boiler. Make sure the work area is orderly and not too crowded.

A handy supply of water—either from a faucet or from a container such as a large pitcher—is needed for the projects that involve melting wax. It's a good idea to keep a clock nearby to gauge time when required in the projects.

Air temperature is an important factor in making a molded candle. If the room is too hot—about 85 degrees F. (29 degrees C.) or above—the wax will cool too slowly, fail to shrink properly, and possibly remain stuck in the mold. If the room is too cold—about 60 degrees F. (16 degrees C.) or below—the wax will cool and shrink too quickly, possibly marring the finish with cracks, fogging, and other blemishes. Let your body's comfort level be your guide.

If a kitchen is not available, a workspace can be created in an area such as the basement or the garage. Projects that involve melting wax require a portable electric hot plate and counter/table setup. Make sure an outlet for electricity is accessible from the work area and that the table is large enough to accommodate all materials and equipment.

Making candles commands your full, uninterrupted attention. If you don't have the amount of time specified at the start of each project, consider postponing the session until time permits.

3

Candle Safety

Keep these tips in mind when making and using candles:

1. Constantly monitor the wax while heating it—do not leave it unattended for even a moment while it is on the burner. If you must leave the room for any reason, remove the wax from the heat.
2. Never heat wax in a container placed directly on a burner, because the temperature of the wax could rise to dangerous levels and pose a fire risk. Always use a double boiler, which ensures that the wax will not reach a temperature greater than 212 degrees F. (100 degrees C.), the boiling point of water.
3. Never melt wax in a microwave oven, because heating is not uniform, and splattering may cause a fire.
4. Do not pour hot wax down the drain, because it could form a stubborn clog in the pipes.
5. Molten wax has the same properties as hot cooking oil. If the wax starts smoking, it is too hot and might catch fire. Remove it from the heat source immediately.
6. Never use water or other liquids to extinguish a wax fire—doing so will spread the flames. Instead, use the lid of a pan or a wet towel to snuff it out.

Household sugar or baking soda, or a chemical fire extinguisher, may be used as well.
7. Use an oven mitt when handling hot pots and other candle making equipment.
8. Do not wear loose-fitting clothing that might touch hot burners. An apron can be worn to protect from hot wax spills and clothing stains. Minor burns should be treated with cold running water.
9. Keep pot handles turned in so they do not stick out over the edge of the work surface.
10. Young children must be supervised while making candles.
11. Keep all candle making supplies—particularly wax remover and fragrance oil—away from children and pets.
12. Make sure candles are placed on a level surface before burning.
13. Never leave lit candles unattended.
14. Keep lit candles a safe distance from any materials that may burn, such as furniture and books or curtains and bedding.
15. Candlewicks should be no longer than $1/8$ to $1/4$ inch. Trim them as needed.
16. Never leave the house or go to bed without extinguishing all candles.

4

Basic Container Candle

Container candles are, simply put, candles that are poured, hardened, and burned in containers. Any jar, cup, bowl, or other vessel that can withstand the rigors of molten liquid and direct, open flame may be used for this kind of candle. In this project, proper amounts of dye and fragrance oil (red dye and cinnamon scent are suggested here) are added to a pound of melted wax and poured into two appropriate, common containers—8-ounce canning jars. The vast selection of dyes, scents, and container types available today ensures that each candle making session can produce a unique result. Recipe amounts can be doubled or halved successfully. This type of candle is the staple of commercial candle outlets and is well known for its characteristically strong aroma even when it's not lit.

While canning jars are recommended for beginners, most craft stores sell a variety of glass containers designed for candle making. In addition, experienced candle makers use many types of sturdy "found items" such as clam or oyster shells, concave stones, or even hollowed-out coconuts for their creations. Some containers, such as the coconut, may burn when exposed to flame, so they are best suited for decorative purposes only. Metal tins may be used only if they are watertight and pose no fire risk. Use common sense when selecting containers.

An easy way to calculate the capacity of any container is to fill it with water, then pour the water into a measuring cup and weigh your wax accordingly.

TIME INVESTMENT
Approximately 2¹/₂ hours uninterrupted,
with 2 to 3 additional hours
of cooling time.

Item		Quantity
❏ Paraffin	(page 2)	1 pound
❏ Stearin	(page 3)	3 tablespoons
❏ Wick	(page 4)	Wire core, one package (matched to suit candle's diameter)
❏ Metal wick tabs	(page 5)	One package
❏ Mold sealer	(page 5)	One package
❏ Containers	(page 9)	Glass, two 8-ounce canning jars
❏ Double boiler	(page 12)	One
❏ Thermometer	(page 13)	One
❏ Kitchen scale	(page 13)	One
❏ Metal pouring jug	(page 13)	Half-gallon capacity recommended
❏ Scissors/knife	(page 14)	One
❏ Dye	(page 6)	One package
❏ Fragance oil	(page 7)	One package/bottle
❏ Wooden spoon	(page 14)	One, at least 12 inches long
❏ Wooden ice cream sticks	(page 14)	At least three
❏ Measuring spoons	(page 15)	One ring
❏ Oven mitts	(page 14)	One pair
❏ Apron	(page 14)	
❏ Newspapers	(page 16)	Enough to cover work area
❏ Paper towels/cleaning rag	(page 16)	
❏ Small plastic bags	(page 17)	Enough to hold unused materials
❏ Empty coffee can	(page 17)	
❏ Candle wax remover	(page 8)	One bottle

If you have difficulty locating materials or equipment in your local craft or department store, find them easily on the Internet. Just log on to your favorite search engine and type "candle making" + "supplies" to contact hundreds of online retailers.

1. Remove small appliances, utensil holders, and other items from the work area so they aren't inadvertently splashed with melted wax.

2. Spread newspapers across countertops in the work area to a thickness of three or four pages. Make sure all surfaces nearby are covered completely.

3. Gather all materials and equipment purchased for the project and place them on the countertop.

4. Remove items from packaging material so they are easily accessible; save packages to store leftover materials, such as dyes and wicks.

5. Check to make sure the equipment is clean and dry.

Dirt and water will adversely affect the quality of the finished candle.

6. Wipe away dirt and moisture from the containers (or mold) with a clean, dry cloth.

Make sure it is not chipped, cracked, or damaged in any way.

7. Add water to the bottom pan of the double boiler until it's half full.

8. Do not overfill. If too much water is added above the midway point of the pan, water might boil over and steam might end up in the top pan with the melted wax. Any candles made with water-contaminated wax will be riddled with imperfections.

9. Make sure the top pan of the double boiler fits without displacing water from the lower pan.

10. The top pan should fit firmly without floating.

11. **WARNING**

The water level in the bottom pan must be monitored to prevent it from running dry, which could allow the wax to reach unsafe temperatures.

12. Place the double boiler on the burner; turn the burner or heating element up to high.

The water should reach the boiling point (212 degrees F., 100 degrees C.) in about 10 minutes.

10 minutes

Container Candle

13. While the water heats, prepare the paraffin. If necessary, break the paraffin into small chunks with a hammer and chisel (or screwdriver).

14. Weigh precisely 1 pound (16 ounces) of paraffin on the kitchen scale.

15. Add the chunks of wax to the top pan of the double boiler.

16. Once the water has reached the boiling point, the wax will begin to melt.

Container Candle

17. Add three level tablespoons of stearin to the wax in the top pan of the double boiler.

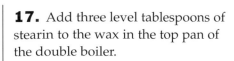

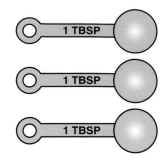

18. If you add too much stearin, the finished candle will take on a soaplike, frosted appearance. If you add too little stearin, the wax might not cool properly and the candle may not burn very well. When making a candle in a mold, adding too little stearin could make the cooled candle difficult to remove from the mold.

19. Expect the stearin-paraffin mixture to melt completely in about 10 minutes; it will reach the desired pouring temperature—180 degrees F. (82 degrees C.)—in 20 to 25 minutes.

10 minutes

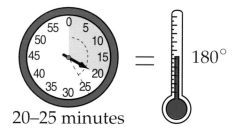

20–25 minutes

20. Stir the wax mixture carefully with a wooden spoon. Avoid splashing the wax, which might cause burns or allow air to become trapped in the wax.

21. Remember to place the wax-covered spoon on an area that is protected by newspapers. This simple step will save considerable cleanup time.

22. <u>**WARNING**</u>
The thermometer can be placed into the wax at this point to monitor the temperature. As long as water remains in the bottom pan of the double boiler, there is no risk of the wax overheating.

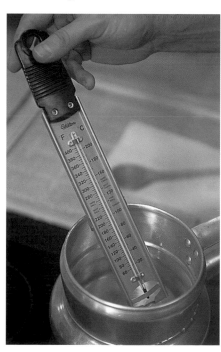

23. While the wax melts, uncoil a strand of wick and, using the glass container as a guide, measure a section that is 2 inches longer than the height of the container.

24. Snip this section of wick with a knife or scissors.

25. Using the first section of wick as a gauge, measure and cut a second segment of wick.

26. The candlewick needs to be "primed"—coated and saturated with wax—before it can be used in a candle. An unprimed wick will burn out extremely fast, much like a piece of cloth would.

To prime the wick, grasp the top section of wick between your thumb and forefinger. Slowly submerge it in the hot wax for 30 seconds. Leave about an inch of wick above the surface of the wax so your fingers do not touch hot wax.

30 seconds

27. After 30 seconds, remove the wick and let excess wax drip back into the double boiler pan. Continue holding the wick in this way for 1 minute, until it has cooled.

1 minute

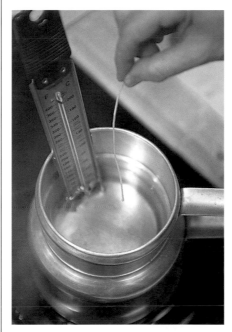

28. After it has cooled, gently run your thumb and forefinger down the length of the wax-covered wick to straighten any bends, curves, or kinks.

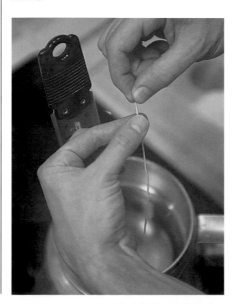

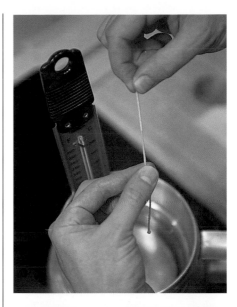

29. Thread a $^{1}/_{2}$-inch section of the unprimed end of the wick through the small hole in a metal wick tab.

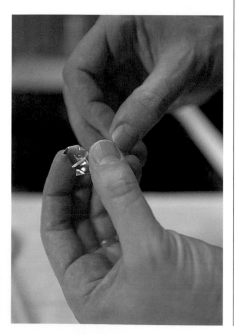

30. Make sure the four sharp "feet" point downward, because they help anchor the wick more firmly in the wax.

31. Use the handle of the wooden spoon to press closed the interior flanges of the tab so the wick is held firmly in place.

32. Straighten the wick and adjust the metal wick tab so it hangs evenly.

33. Repeat for the other section of wick.

34. Take a nickel-size chunk of mold sealer and press it firmly onto the bottom of the jar. Make sure it is centered, because it will hold the wick tab and wick in place.

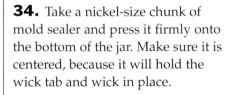

35. Press the wick tab into the sealer.

Use your index finger to press firmly.

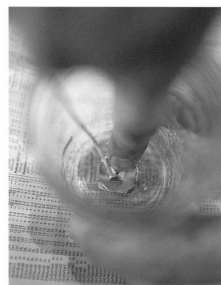

36. When the wax and stearin have liquefied, add the dye. Follow the manufacturer's directions for proper amounts, usually about $^1/_8$ to $^1/_4$ ounce per pound of paraffin.

1/8 oz.　　　to

1/4 oz.

37. Remember to add dye amounts gradually; more dye can be added later, but it can't be removed once it's added.

38. Stir the wax and dye carefully until it's well blended. The wax will have the appearance of colored water at this point. Remember, the color will become more vivid and dense when the wax cools.

39. Now is the time to test the color of the hot wax. Use the wooden spoon to place a few drops of wax on a paper towel. Wait for the wax to cool, and make sure the color depth is to your liking.

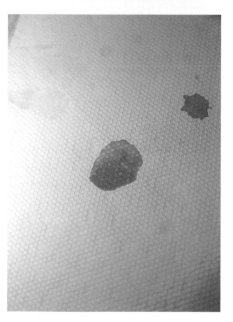

40. If the color is too weak, add a little more dye to the pan of melted wax.

41. Stir slowly after adding dye until blended. Test the color again. Repeat as needed until the desired color is attained.

42. Add fragrance to the wax according to the manufacturer's directions, usually $1/8$ to $1/4$ ounce of oil per pound of wax, or slightly more for powdered fragrance.

| 1/8 oz. | to |
| 1/4 oz. | |

Stir until well blended.

43. Prepare the glass jars for pouring by setting them near the heat of the burner and double boiler. Warming the glass helps to eliminate air bubbles and streaks that could result from stark temperature contrasts between the glass and the wax.

44. When the temperature reaches 180 degrees F. (82 degrees C.), it's time to fill the glass container.

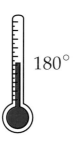

180°

Remove the thermometer from the wax.

45. Turn off the burner.

46.

Oven mitts may be needed at this point if the handle of the boiler pan is too hot.

47. Lift out the top pan of the double boiler.

48. Over the newspaper-covered work area, pour the wax from the pan into the metal pouring can slowly and carefully. Slow and steady pouring is the key to this step, like pouring a cup of hot coffee or tea. Tilt the jug so the wax does not splash off the bottom and create air bubbles that might ruin the candle's finish.

49. Slowly pour the wax into the jars, resting the rim of the pouring jug on the jar for greater control. A steady pour in the center works well. Fill to within $1/2$ inch of the top so there is some wax left in reserve for an additional pouring that will be needed as the candle cools.

Container Candle

50. Return unused wax to the top pan of the double boiler. It will be used once the candle has begun to harden in about an hour.

51. Grasp the wick gently with one hand. Take a wooden ice cream stick in the other and place it horizontally across the center of one jar.

52. Loop the end of the wick around the stick one time.

Here's a closer look at the proper technique for looping the wick around the wooden stick.

53. The primed wick should be stiff enough to grip the stick once it is looped.

If it appears loose, use a small piece of mold sealer to hold it in place.

54. Make sure the wick remains taut, with no bends or slack parts.
Repeat the wick procedure on the second candle.

55. Slide the loop along the stick until the wick is centered inside the mold. This is important, because a candle will not burn evenly if the wick is too close to the side.

56. Take the spoon and firmly tap against the sides of the glass container to dislodge any air bubbles trapped in the molten wax. After tapping, check to make sure the wick remains centered.

57. The remaining steps of this project require patience, because it takes time to cool molten wax. The wax will cool from the outside inward and from the bottom to the top—meaning the core of the candle will remain liquid the longest.

58. About 15 minutes after pouring, the cooling wax will begin to turn opaque in the mold, and a thin skin will form on the surface. Keep in mind that wax will cool more quickly in smaller molds than in larger molds.

15 minutes

59. The wax will then begin shrinking down into the candle as it cools, leaving an indented well around the wick.

Container Candle

60. After 30 minutes, gently pierce the skin of the candle with an ice cream stick to release air trapped in the candle.

30 minutes

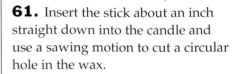

WARNING

Don't poke too rapidly; the central core of the candle is still liquid, and molten wax may accidentally squirt out if the stick is inserted too quickly.

61. Insert the stick about an inch straight down into the candle and use a sawing motion to cut a circular hole in the wax.

62. Failure to punch holes in the skin now will allow trapped air to form a pocket in the center of the candle and make it impossible to burn.

63. Allow the candle to cool for 30 more minutes.

30 minutes

64.

Check the water level in the bottom pan of the double boiler and refill if necessary.

Turn the heating element to high.

Remelt the wax in the double boiler. It will take about 15 minutes to reach the proper pouring temperature of 180 degrees F. (82 degrees C.).

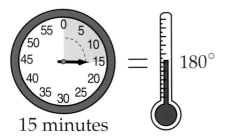

15 minutes

65. Pierce the surface of the cooling wax in the mold a final time to release air.

66. When the wax reaches the proper temperature, carefully transfer it from the double boiler into the metal pouring can.

Turn off the heat.

67. Carefully and slowly pour the wax into the cavity in the candle. Fill to the level of the original pour.

68. In most cases, this second pour—also called "topping off"—is the last step that involves hot wax. Several intangibles, such as slow or uneven cooling, could cause the wax to shrink significantly one last time. Any formation of an indentation will be visible after about 20 minutes of cooling. If needed, reheat the wax in the double boiler to 180 degrees F. (82 degrees C.) and re-pour to the original level.

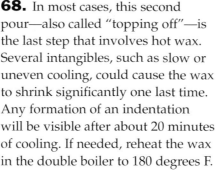

69. Pour the remaining wax into a coffee can or similar container for use later.

70. Let the candle cool to room temperature for 2 to 3 hours.

2–3 hours

71. For a quicker cooldown, the candle may be placed in the refrigerator for about an hour, or it can be placed in a basin full of cool water—known as a "water bath"—for about an hour or so.

Never cool a candle in the freezer, because the drastic temperature change will cause the wax to crack.

72. While waiting for the candle to cool, clean up the work area and the equipment.

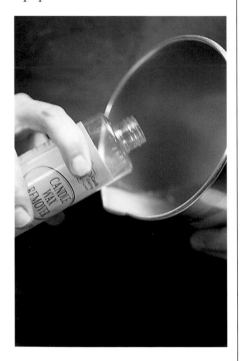

73. Once the candle has cooled undo the loop in the wick and remove the wooden stick.

74. Trim the excess wick to between $1/4$ and $1/2$ inch. For best results, let the candle set for at least 24 hours before burning.

24 hours

TIPS

- **To increase the burning time** of any candle, place it in the refrigerator for an hour prior to burning. This makes the wax denser and allows the candle to burn longer.

- **Many containers can be** refilled once the candle has burned down. Close inspection must be made, though, to ensure that the container is not chipped or damaged from the heat of the first candle.

In addition to the nearly limitless combinations of colors, scents, and containers available to the candle maker, a few simple variations on each project can produce a wide range of effects. Most of these modifications require only basic skills.

Two-tone layer candle

This candle requires two separate batches of wax, each a different color. Pour the first batch into the container, filling it about halfway up. Allow this layer to cool partially until it has a spongy consistency. Heat and pour a second batch on top of the first, creating the two-tone look. Some practice is needed to master this technique.

Using the same technique with additional batches of wax, multilayered candles of numerous colors can be created.

Angled layer candle

This is an even more difficult variation. Create this layer candle by tilting the container, pouring wax, and allowing it to harden at an angle. The effect can be dramatic.

"Top-up" votives

These candles are just like miniature versions of container candles, with one primary difference—the candle doesn't stay in the small container in which it hardened.

Instead, the votive is removed and placed into a different holder for burning, usually a small glass or metal cup that supports the candle. Other kinds of holders include terra-cotta pots or ceramic cups designed to withstand direct flame.

Remember to use wire core wicks and metal wick tabs for this type of candle. A 1-pound batch of wax can produce about a dozen votives.

Tea light candles

The smallest of all container candles, tea lights are used to heat liquid potpourri and to illuminate ornamental candle holders. Wire core wick and metal containers, available at craft stores, should be used in tea light candles.

Container Candle

5

Basic Molded Candle

Molded pillars are perhaps the stateliest of all candles. They take on the shape of whatever mold the hot wax is poured into; pillars can be made that stand several feet tall. In this project, proper amounts of dye and fragrance oil (white dye and vanilla scent are suggested here) are added to 1 pound of melted wax and poured into a rigid plastic mold 7 inches high and 2 inches in diameter.

Keep in mind that recipe amounts can be doubled or halved successfully. An easy way to calculate the capacity of any mold is to fill it with water, then pour the water into a measuring cup and weigh your wax accordingly. Remember that 16 ounces equals a pound. Make sure the mold is completely dry before filling it with wax, because water can mar the surface. A molded pillar candle can be used as a table centerpiece or general decoration throughout the home.

TIME INVESTMENT
Approximately 2¹/₂ hours uninterrupted,
with 2 to 3 additional hours
of cooling time.

SHOPPING LIST: Basic Molded Candle

Item		Quantity
❑ Paraffin	(page 2)	1 pound
❑ Stearin	(page 3)	3 tablespoons
❑ Wick	(page 4)	Cotton core, one package
		(matched to suit candle's diameter)
❑ Mold sealer	(page 5)	One package
❑ Candle mold	(page 10)	Plastic, 7 inches high by 2 inches in diameter
❑ Double boiler	(page 12)	One
❑ Thermometer	(page 13)	One
❑ Kitchen scale	(page 13)	One
❑ Metal pouring jug	(page 13)	Half-gallon capacity recommended
❑ Scissors/knife	(page 14)	One
❑ Dye	(page 6)	One package
❑ Fragance oil	(page 7)	One package/bottle
❑ Wooden spoon	(page 14)	One, at least 12 inches long
❑ Wooden ice cream sticks	(page 14)	At least two
❑ Measuring spoons	(page 15)	One ring
❑ Oven mitts	(page 14)	One pair
❑ Apron	(page 14)	
❑ Newspapers	(page 16)	Enough to cover work area
❑ Paper towels/cleaning rag	(page 16)	
❑ Small plastic bags	(page 17)	Enough to hold unused materials
❑ Empty coffee can	(page 17)	
❑ Candle wax remover	(page 8)	One bottle

If you have difficulty locating materials or equipment in your local craft or department store, find them easily on the Internet. Just log on to your favorite search engine and type "candle making" + "supplies" to contact hundreds of online retailers.

Follow Steps 1 to 22 of the Basic Container Candle Project (pages 23 to 27), which explain the proper way to prepare the work area and equipment, weigh and melt paraffin, and add stearin.

23. While the wax melts, uncoil a strand of wick and, using the mold as a guide, measure a section that is about 3 inches longer than the height of the container.

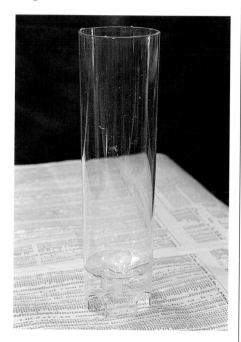

24. Snip this section of wick with a knife or scissors.

25. The candlewick needs to be "primed"—coated and saturated with wax—before it can be used in a candle; otherwise it will burn too quickly. Grasp the section of wick between your thumb and forefinger. Slowly submerge it in the hot wax for 30 seconds. Leave about an inch of wick above the surface of the wax so your fingers do not touch hot wax.

30 seconds

26. After 30 seconds, remove the wick and let excess wax drip back into the double boiler pan. Continue holding the wick in this way for 1 minute, until it has cooled.

1 minute

27. Gently run your thumb and forefinger down the length of the wax-covered wick to straighten any bends, curves, or kinks.

28. Thread the wick, unprimed end first, through the small hole in the bottom of the mold.

29. Feed the wick into the mold until the unprimed end of wick reaches the large opening. Grasp this section and gently pull the wick until no more than 1 inch protrudes from the small hole in the mold. Remember, this "bottom" part of the mold will contain the top of the finished candle, and the wick will need to be trimmed further before the candle can be burned.

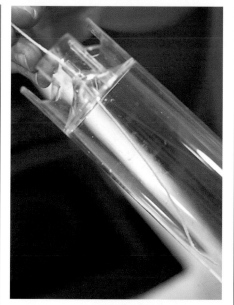

30. Press the wick down at a right angle. It will be stiff enough to stay in place on its own.

31. Place the mold on the counter-top so that it is level. The mold can rest for the moment on top of the unprimed section of wick protruding from the large opening.

32. Take a clump of mold sealer and tear off a wad about the size of a piece of chewed bubble gum.

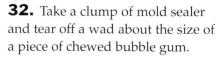

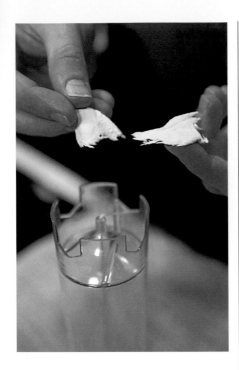

33. Press until the piece is flat and smooth and is about ¼ inch thick. Make sure the piece is firm, with no air pockets or thin spots that might allow hot wax to seep through it.

34. Place the piece over the bent wick and hole. Press down firmly against the plastic to seal tightly. Make sure the sealer covers the hole/wick uniformly.

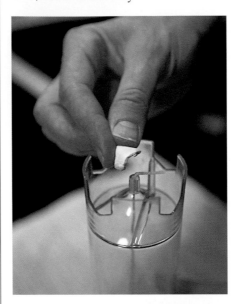

35. Add a second wad of sealer and press into place. Remember, too much mold sealer is far better than too little when hot wax is involved.

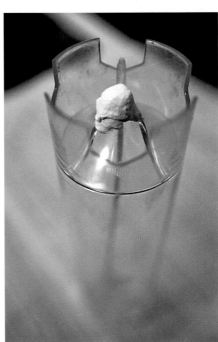

36. Turn the mold over so the large opening is at the top, and set it on the level countertop.

37. Pull the wick up so that it becomes taut.

38. Take a wooden ice cream stick
and wrap the wick around it.

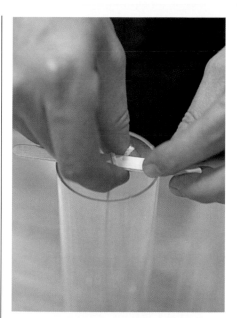

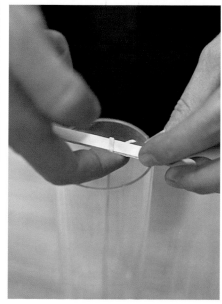

39. Use a small piece of mold sealer to hold the looped wick in place, if needed. Keep the wick taut—no bends—and centered in the mold.

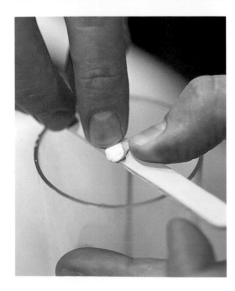

40. When the wax and stearin have liquefied properly, add the dye. Follow the manufacturer's directions for proper amounts, usually about ¹/₈ to ¹/₄ ounce per pound of paraffin.

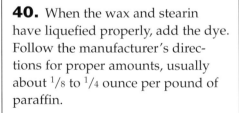

1/8 oz.

to

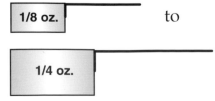

1/4 oz.

41. Remember to add dye amounts gradually; more dye can be added later, but it can't be removed once it's added.

42. Stir the wax and dye carefully until well blended. The wax will have the appearance of colored water at this point. Remember, the color will become more vivid and dense when the wax cools.

43. Now is the time to test the color of the hot wax. Use the wooden spoon to place a few drops of wax on a paper towel. Wait for the wax to cool, and make sure the color depth is to your liking.

In the case of white dye, use a piece of plastic or a dark-colored surface to make the color of the wax stand out.

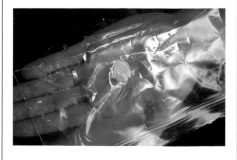

44. If the color is too weak, add a little more dye to the pan of melted wax.

45. Stir slowly after adding dye until blended. Test the color again. Repeat as needed until the proper color is attained.

46. Add fragrance to the wax according to the manufacturer's directions, usually $1/8$ to $1/4$ ounce of oil per pound of wax, or slightly more for powdered fragrance.

| 1/8 oz. | to |
| 1/4 oz. | |

Stir to blend thoroughly.

47. Make sure the thermometer has been placed into the wax.

48. When the temperature reaches 180 degrees F. (82 degrees C.), it's time to fill the plastic mold.

49. Turn off the burner.

50. Lift out the top pan of the double boiler. Oven mitts may be needed at this point if the handle is too hot.

Slowly and carefully transfer the wax from the pan into the metal pouring can. Work over an area covered with newspapers. Pour steadily to prevent the wax from splashing; too much agitation might trap air bubbles in the wax, which could affect the quality of the candle.

51. Tilting the mold slightly can decrease agitation. Pour steadily until the mold is filled to within about $1/2$ inch of the top.

52. Make sure the wick has remained taut and centered inside the mold. This is important, because a candle will not burn evenly if the wick is too close to either side.

53. Return unused wax to the top pan of the double boiler. It will be used shortly to refill the mold as the candle shrinks and cools.

54. Check the water level of the double boiler now.

55. Tap sharply against the mold with a spoon to free air bubbles trapped in the wax. When finished, check to see that the wick is centered.

56. Now it's time to let the wax cool. The outside of the candle will harden first; the core takes longer.

57. About 15 minutes after pouring, the cooling wax will begin to solidify. As it does, a film will form on the surface of the wax at the top of the mold.

15 minutes

58. As it cools, the hot wax will contract. This will cause a depression to form in the candle around the wick.

59. A pocket of air becomes trapped inside the candle after about 30 minutes. Use an ice cream stick to poke into the candle to release the air.

30 minutes

WARNING

Don't poke with too much force, because hot wax may accidentally squirt from the core of the candle.

60. Insert the stick about 1 inch straight down into the candle and use a sawing motion to cut a circular hole in the wax.

61. Failure to punch holes in the skin now will allow trapped air to form a pocket in the center of the candle and make it impossible to burn.

62. Allow the candle to cool for 30 more minutes.

30 minutes

63. Turn the heating element to high and remelt the wax in the double boiler. It will take about 15 minutes to reach the proper pouring temperature of 180 degrees F. (82 degrees C.).

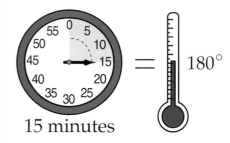

15 minutes

64. Pierce the surface of the cooling wax in the mold a final time to release air.

65. When the wax reaches the proper temperature, transfer it from the double boiler into the metal pouring can.

66.

Pour the wax into the well that has formed in the candle. Do not overfill the candle, because hot wax might spill over the edge, seep between the candle and the mold, and make it very difficult to remove the candle when cooled.

69. Let the candle cool to room temperature for about 3 to 4 hours or, even better, overnight. The mold on a properly cooled candle will not be warm to the touch.

3–4 hours = Good

24 hours = Recommended

67. This second pour is usually the last one needed. Candles made in extremely large molds that hold several pounds of wax may require subsequent pours. Simply check to see if a significant indentation is forming, and if so, refill the candle. Remember not to fill the candle above the level of the original pour.

68. Transfer the unused wax into a coffee can or similar storage container.

70. The candle may be placed in the refrigerator to speed cooling. This method usually takes an hour or two, depending on the size of the mold used. The mold also can be placed upright in a basin of cool water for an hour or so. Make sure the water level isn't higher than the mold. Use a small weight to keep the mold submerged if needed.

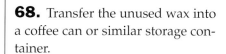

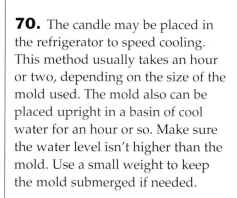

71. WARNING
Never cool a candle in the freezer, because the drastic temperature change will cause the wax to crack.

72. Clean up the work area and the equipment.

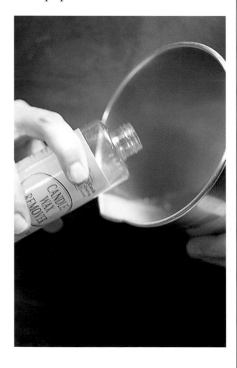

73. Once the candle has cooled, unloop the wick, remove the small bit of mold sealer, and remove the wooden stick.

74. Turn the candle over and remove the large lump of mold sealer. Make sure all the mold sealer is removed from this part of the wick, because it might clog the wick and affect burning. Sealer is reusable.

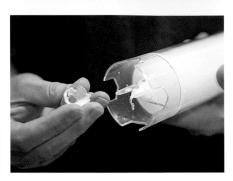

75. Make sure the wick is straight.

76. Grasp the section of wick at the bottom of the mold, gently tug it, and remove the hardened candle.

77. **WARNING**

If the candle sticks in the mold, gently squeeze it a few times or lightly rap it on the countertop. Do not use too much force, or the mold might crack.

78. If both of these methods fail, stick the mold in the refrigerator overnight. The wax should contract more and allow for the candle's removal.

If the candle still refuses to come out of the mold using the steps outlined, the candle is most likely ruined. Unfortunately, the mold and candle must be placed in the double boiler. Heat until the wax melts from the mold and repour.

79. Trim the excess wick on the bottom of the candle as flush as possible.

80. If the bottom of the candle is uneven, turn the burner to high and allow the double boiler to heat up.

81. When hot, place the bottom of the candle in the top pan of the double boiler. Press down firmly, and keep the candle as level as possible. Wax should melt off the bottom of the candle instantly and spread out in the pan.

82. Slide the bottom of the candle across the hot pan in a circular motion, keeping it level to the pan. The process is a fast one, usually taking no more than 30 seconds to complete once the pan is hot.

83. Check the bottom of the candle for evenness. Repeat if necessary.

84. When the bottom has cooled—in about a minute—trim the wick at the top of the candle to between $^1/_4$ and $^1/_2$ inch.

For best results, allow the candle to set for at least 24 hours before burning.

24 hours

Save or discard the small amount of wax remaining in the double boiler pan.

TIP

• **Any blemish or imperfection** left on the surface of the candle can be buffed out using a nylon stocking. This technique also can be used to polish a dull finish on a candle.

Basic Molded Candle Variations

These are based on skills learned in the basic molded candle project.

Votives

Votive candles made in the "top-down" style are much smaller than typical pillar candles, so each batch of wax can produce more candles. Primed wire core wick needs to be threaded through the small hole in the bottom of each cup, and mold sealer must be applied around the hole and wick—the same as detailed in the main project.

Votives must be placed into a holder for burning, usually a small glass or metal cup that supports the candle (see "Top-up votives," page 45). Other kinds of holders include terra-cotta pots and ceramic cups designed to withstand direct flame.

Ice candle

Place a finished pillar candle into a larger mold of any shape, making sure the wick protrudes from the small hole in the mold. Pack chipped pieces of ice around the candle. Use an oven mitt to hold the mold over a basin of water and pour hot wax into it. The ice will harden the wax on contact, and a new candle will form that contains contours and pockets left by the ice. The size of the ice chips dictates the size of the indentations. Make sure the wick hole is not plugged, because water from the melted ice needs a way out of the mold. Once the candle has cooled, turn the mold over and shake out any remaining water. Allow the candle to dry thoroughly before lighting, or the flame will sputter. Making an ice candle is tricky and takes practice to master.

Mineral oil candle

Follow the basic directions above, except add mineral oil to the wax prior to pouring. Several tablespoons will create an unusual sheen on the surface of the finished candle. Experiment with varying amounts of oil for different effects.

Two-tone layer pillar

Follow instructions on page 45 for making a two-tone layer candle in a container.

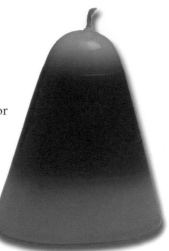

Angled layer candle

Follow instructions on page 45 for making an angled layer candle.

Appliqué candles

Appliqué wax can be used as glue to apply a variety of materials to the outside of the finished candle to enhance its look. These materials include small shells and stones, metal beads, dried flowers or leaves, ribbons or cloth swatches, mirrored tiles, and gem-like chunks of glass.

This wax also helps glitter and similar materials stick to the candle.

Because many of these items are flammable, common sense dictates that most adorned candles should be used only for decoration and should not be lit.

Painted candles

The budding artist can brush poster or craft paint onto the finished candle to good effect. Some paints contain chemicals that may be unsafe when burned, so check the ingredients on the label before lighting.

Dripped candle

Place a finished candle on a covered work area.

Light a taper candle.

Hold the taper about an inch or two above the finished candle. Tilt the taper until the flame makes contact with the wax at the tip. This will accelerate the melting process.

Allow the wax to drip down the sides of the finished candle, creating streaks of color from top to bottom. Periodically change the position of the taper so drip lines encircle the candle.

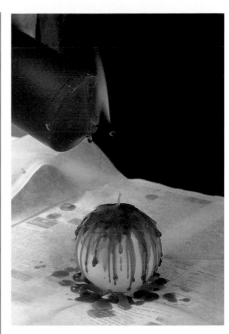

TIP

- **Candles with unusual** shapes, such as balls and ovals, are a good choice for this variation, because the wax will flow easily down the sides. Straight-sided candles should be held at an angle to produce a proper dripped effect.

6

Basic Dipped Candle

The dipped taper candle is relatively easy to make, requiring mainly elbow grease and time to build up layer upon layer of wax.

The specific amount of paraffin needed for this project depends on the capacity of the metal container you use for dipping. Keep in mind that the depth of the melted wax in the container will determine the length of the finished pair of candles, which are joined by the uncut wick. Simply put, shorter candles require a smaller container, and larger candles require a larger container. Because a sizable quantity of melted wax is needed to fill a normal container, dipped candles usually are made in large batches to avoid excessive waste.

For the project illustrated here, about 4 pounds of wax was added to a metal pouring jug with a capacity of 1 gallon. This is enough to make a dozen 7-inch-tall tapers.

Unlike the two other hot wax projects in the book, no stearin needs to be added to the paraffin used to make dipped candles. The wax does not need to be hardened or made more opaque, because a heavy concentration of dye is used to finish the candle.

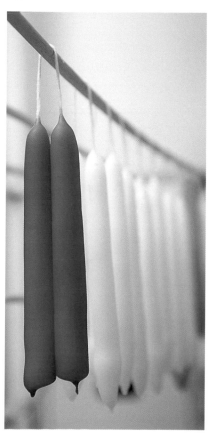

TIME INVESTMENT
Approximately 3 hours uninterrupted,
with 2 to 3 additional hours
of cooling time.

SHOPPING LIST: Basic Dipped Candle

Item		Quantity
❏ Paraffin	(page 2)	Enough to fill dipping container
❏ Wick	(page 4)	Cotton core, one package
		(suited for candles of 1-inch diameter or less)
❏ Double boiler	(page 12)	One
❏ Thermometer	(page 13)	One
❏ Dipping container	(page 13)	Metal pouring jug recommended
❏ Scissors/knife	(page 14)	One
❏ Dye	(page 6)	About $1/2$ ounce per pound of wax
		(for overdipping candle)
❏ Wooden spoon	(page 14)	One, at least 12 inches long
❏ Wooden drying rack	(page 15)	One
❏ Oven mitts	(page 14)	One pair
❏ Apron	(page 14)	
❏ Newspapers	(page 16)	Enough to cover work area
❏ Paper towels/cleaning rag	(page 16)	
❏ Small plastic bags	(page 17)	Enough to hold unused materials
❏ Wax paper	(page 16)	
❏ Empty coffee can	(page 17)	
❏ Candle wax remover	(page 8)	One bottle

If you have difficulty locating materials or equipment in your local craft or department store, find them easily on the Internet. Just log on to your favorite search engine and type "candle making" + "supplies" to contact hundreds of online retailers.

1. Spread newspapers across countertops in the work area to a thickness of three or four pages.

2. Make sure all surfaces nearby are covered completely.

3. Spread newspapers on the floor and set up the drying rack on top of them. Make sure the rack is within easy reach of the dipping container so candles can be hung quickly to cool.

4. Gather materials and equipment purchased for the project and place them in the work area.

5. Remove items from packaging material so they are easy to access; save packages to store leftover materials, such as dyes and wicks. Plastic sandwich bags are also good for storing unused supplies.

6. Check to make sure the equipment is clean and dry; dirt and water in the dipping container or top double boiler pan can ruin the finished candle.

7. Add water to the bottom pan of the double boiler until half full. Don't overfill, because the water might boil over and splash into the wax, which will ruin the candles.

8.
Check the water level in the bottom pan occasionally and add water as needed. Wax can reach unsafe temperatures if the bottom pan is allowed to run dry while on the burner.

9. Turn the burner up to high.

10. The water should reach the boiling point (212 degrees F., 100 degrees C.) in about 10 minutes.

 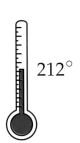 212°

10 minutes

11. As the water heats, add several chunks of paraffin to the dipping container.

Break larger pieces of paraffin into smaller chunks using a hammer and chisel (or screwdriver).

Do not allow wax to stick out above the lip of the container, because melted wax might drip onto the heating element and present a fire hazard.

12. Once the water has reached the boiling point, the wax will begin melting.

A 1-gallon dipping container can hold about 5 pounds of paraffin, which reaches the desired dipping temperature—160 degrees F. (71 degrees C.)—in 15 to 20 minutes.

15–20 minutes

13. Remember, the depth of the wax dictates the height of the candle. Keep at least 1 pound of wax chunks in reserve to raise the level of wax in the container as needed during dipping.

14. While the wax is melting, use a ruler to measure the height of the dipping can.

15. Measure a section of wick that is 4 inches longer than the height of the container.

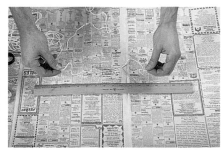

16. Double the segment of wick on itself; snip this section of wick with a knife or scissors. Remember, dipped candles are made in pairs.

17. Use this piece of wick as a guide to measure 11 additional sections of wick the same length. Set them aside.

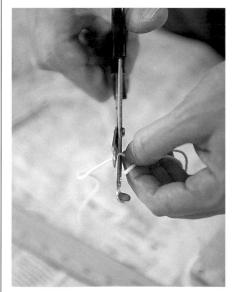

18. Place the thermometer into the wax.

19. Heat the paraffin to 160 degrees F. (71 degrees C.).

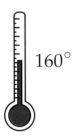

160°

20. When the wax reaches the target temperature, turn off the burner.

TIPS

- **Wax that is too hot—above** 160 degrees F. (71 degrees C.)—will not adhere properly to the wick and will continue to melt back into the pan with each dip. If wax does become too hot, simply wait several minutes for it to cool.

- **As the wax becomes cooler** and cooler, it will adhere to the wick in larger quantities. Do not, however, allow the wax to become too cool—too close to the melting point of the wax—because it will clump unevenly on the candle. If the wax in the container becomes milky or translucent, or if a thin skin begins to form on the surface, it is too cool. Stop dipping and reheat the wax to 160 degrees F. (71 degrees C.).

21. Candles can be dipped using the bare hand, or a simple handle for the wick can be fashioned out of a wooden ice cream stick.

22. To do this, use scissors to cut two small notches about an inch from either end of the stick.

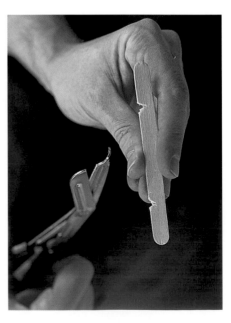

23. Place a section of wick in one notch, loop the strand around the stick, and run the remaining piece of wick into the second notch.

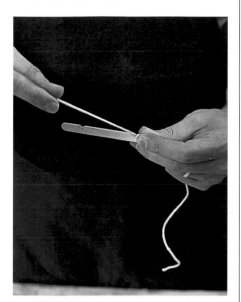

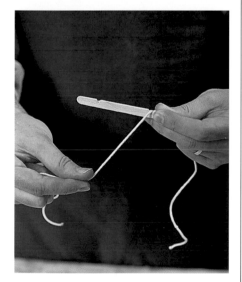

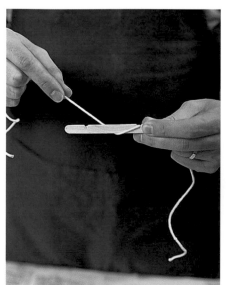

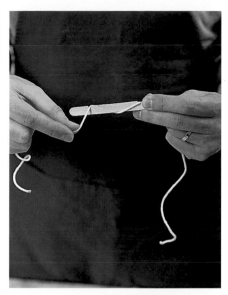

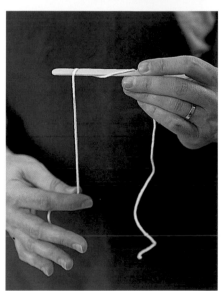

24. Make sure the wick hangs evenly on both sides.

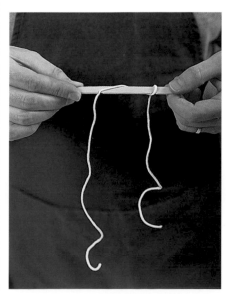

25. Grasp the center of a wick section with thumb and forefinger. Let the two wick tips hang down evenly, and dip them into the wax. Keep the two sections submerged for about a minute, so wax can soak into the wick.

1 minute

26. This first dip lasts the longest; all other dips last no longer than 2 to 3 seconds each.

2–3 seconds

Lift the wick straight up and out of the wax and let excess wax drip back into the container for several seconds.

27. If the two strands of wick touch together and stick, simply slide a finger between them to separate. Don't worry at this point about blemishes in the finish. Subsequent dips will smooth out rough spots.

28. Hold the strand for about 30 seconds until cool.

30 seconds

29. Gently run your thumb and forefinger down the length of the wax-covered wick to straighten any bends, curves, or kinks.

Some candle makers tie small weights, such as metal washers, to each end of wick to keep them hanging straight.

This step is not necessary, because wax naturally beads at the end of the wick. After several dips, the built-up wax alone will be heavy enough to keep the wick straight.

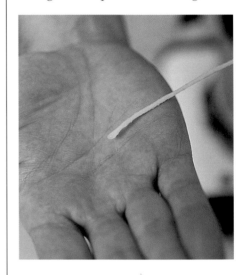

30. Drape the wick over the drying rack.

31. Repeat the soaking steps with the remaining eleven sections of wick.

Keep each wick in order on the rack so that subsequent dips are done in proper sequence.

32. Continue dipping the wick sections one after the other, much like a manufacturing production line, because the first candle in line will be ready to be dipped when the twelfth candle comes out of the wax. For best results, do not allow candles to cool for more than 15 minutes between dips, or they could crack when submerged again in hot wax.

33. When dipping, dunk the candle into the wax and hold submerged for 2 to 3 seconds. Pull the candle out quickly and smoothly in one motion. Allow to cool for at least 1 minute between dips, or the wax will not have time to harden and will become lumpy.

1 minute

34. The wick will begin to take on the classic taper shape—albeit very thin—after five to ten dips. Keep an eye on the wax level at this point.

35. Add more wax chunks as needed.

36. Turn on the heat.

The new chunks will melt in about 10 minutes.

10 minutes

37.

Continue dipping the candles in turn, and add and melt more wax as needed. Remember to check the water level in the double boiler to keep it from going dry.

38. The candles will reach the standard diameter of $^1/_2$ inch in thirty to forty dips, depending on the average temperature of the wax during dipping.

39. Stop dipping when the candles reach the desired thickness.

40. Some candle makers like their dipped tapers to look rough and functional, authentic reminders of the past. For them, the dipped candle is finished at this point and is ready to be hung to cool.

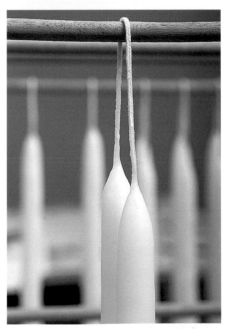

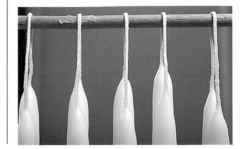

41. Others prefer a smoother finish and a more colorful appearance.

Spread a sheet of wax paper on the work surface in preparation for rolling, which will remove lumps and blemishes from the candle.

42. The candles will be warm all the way through, making them flexible and malleable.

43. Press down on one of the tapers with your fingers. Roll the candle with the fingers using a back and forth motion, like rolling out a piece of dough. The candle will be smooth and even after about 30 seconds of rolling.

44. While the candle is still warm, the bottom can be evened by snipping off excess wax.

45. To complete the project with a vivid touch of color, "overdip" the candle in dye. This step requires more candle dye than any of the other projects in this book, because coloring in the final layer of wax must be dark and dense enough to cover the white paraffin layers under it. Expect to use up to four times as much dye as needed for either a container candle or a poured candle in a mold. In the project illustrated, the dipping container holds 4 pounds of wax. About 2 ounces of commercial dye is needed to properly color the tapers.

46. Turn the burner to high. Heat the wax to 180 degrees F. (82 degrees C.); this hotter temperature will increase surface gloss after the final dip. The wax will reach the target temperature in about 15 minutes.

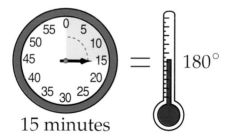

15 minutes

47. Add wax chunks to the dipping container to increase the level if needed. Use enough wax to ensure that the entire candle will be submerged when dipped.

48. As the wax melts, add dye.

49. After adding the dye, stir well to blend.

50. When the temperature has reached 180 degrees F. (82 degrees C.), dip the tapers.

Up to four separate dips might be needed to produce vividly colored candles.

51. Roll the finished candles until smooth.

52. Hang to cool thoroughly. Dipped candles should be allowed to set for 24 hours before burning.

24 hours

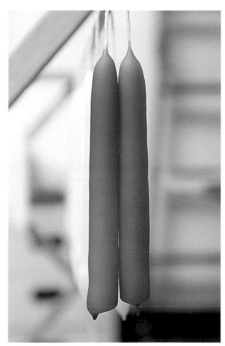

The color difference between the inner core of wax and the new outer layer will be apparent when the candle is burned.

These modifications require only basic skills.

Overdipped pillar or votive

This is the same technique used to overdip a taper as detailed at the end of the dipped taper project. Substitute a pillar or votive for a taper candle and submerge it in wax of a different color.

If needed, use a sturdy clamp or pliers to hold heavier pillar candles during dipping.

The new color will adhere to the candle in layers that thicken with each subsequent dip. A new layer of wax will change from liquid to solid within a minute, but multiple layers need at least 30 minutes of cooling so they can set properly.

Dip using a slow, steady motion to allow the wax to adhere smoothly and to avoid splashing.

The color difference between the inner core and the outer will be apparent when the candle is burned.

Overdipped and engraved

For this variation, a fork, knife, awl, or other sharp implement is needed.

Follow the steps for the overdipped pillar or votive candle variation.

Dip the candle no more than four times in the wax. The key is to create a new layer on the candle without making it too thick, because you must be able to slice through it.

Take the implement and carefully scrape off the new outer layer in a pattern or design to reveal the color underneath. This can be tricky and requires some practice to master.

Twisted tapers

While the wax is still warm, simply twist the top half of the candle down and back up, making a loop near the middle of the candle.

Flattened, twisted taper

For this variation, a rolling pin is needed.

Place a still-warm pair of candles—or a single candle that has been separated—on wax paper and flatten with the rolling pin, in much the same way that dough is rolled.

Begin at the tip of a single candle, and press down firmly until the rolling pin comes to within ¹/₂ inch of the bottom. The bottom itself should not be flattened, so the candle can be placed in a candlestick.

Carefully peel the candle off the wax paper. Straighten out any curves or bends.

Grasp the top and bottom of the candle and twist firmly in opposite directions.

Spirals like the threads on a screw will form after the first twist.

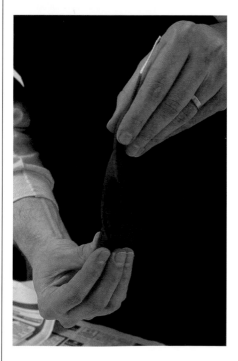

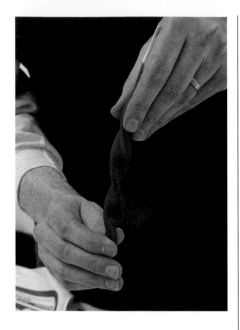

Additional twists will create more spirals.

Extremely tight spirals are formed after many twists.

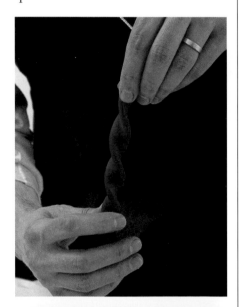

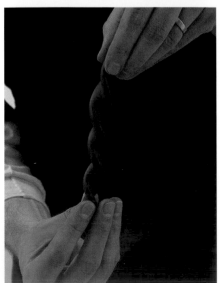

Repeat on the second candle.
Surface blemishes can be covered with a final dip in the hot, colored wax.

Allow candles to cool.

Side-by-side twisted tapers

Take two still-warm tapers and hold them side by side. Make sure the two candles are equal in length. Trim if necessary.

Hold the candles together with one hand and twist the tops with the other.

The candles will entwine, creating an effect that resembles a cruller pastry or a barber pole.

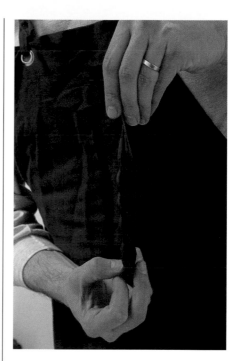

Surface blemishes can be covered with a final dip in the hot, colored wax.

Allow candles to cool.

7

Basic Rolled Beeswax Candle

Rolled beeswax candles are among the easiest to make because they require no melted wax, no fragrance oil, and no commercial dyes. The sweet-scented wax produced by bees comes in ready-to-use sheets that simply need to be cut and rolled properly around a central wick, usually of cotton core construction. At room temperature, beeswax sheets are slightly tacky and pliable; a sharp craft knife will cut through them easily. Under cooler conditions, though, sheets may become stiff and brittle. A hair dryer can be used for a few seconds to heat cold sheets and make them flexible enough to roll successfully. Once rolled, beeswax candles can be easily crushed and damaged, so it's a good idea to place them in a candle holder or a safe area immediately after completion.

TIME INVESTMENT
About 30 to 60 minutes.

Item		Quantity
❏ Beeswax sheet	(page 8)	One, usually sold in packages of three sheets
❏ Wick	(page 4)	Cotton core, one package (suited for candles of 1-inch diameter or less)
❏ Smooth cutting board/ place mat	(page 15)	One
❏ Scissors/knife	(page 14)	One
❏ Hair dryer	(page 15	One
❏ Ruler or straightedge	(page 15)	One
❏ Small plastic bags	(page 17)	Enough to hold unused materials

If you have difficulty locating materials or equipment in your local craft or department store, find them easily on the Internet. Just log on to your favorite search engine and type "candle making" + "supplies" to contact hundreds of online retailers.

Rolled Beeswax Candle

1. Gather materials and equipment purchased for the project and place them on the work surface.

2. Make sure the cutting board / place mat and your hands are clean.

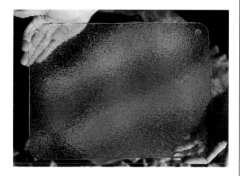

3. Place a single beeswax sheet onto the cutting board with the wide side facing you. This sheet needs to be cut into two equal pieces.

4. Use a ruler to measure the width of the sheet. In the example shown, the sheet is 16 1/2 inches wide, a standard size for beeswax.

5. Determine the middle point of the sheet by dividing the width in half. In the example shown, the center of sheet falls at 8 1/4 inches.

6. Use the craft knife to cut a small perpendicular notch in the sheet at the middle point.

7. Turn the ruler at a right angle so that it is perpendicular to the wide side, and align it over the notch.

8. Make sure the ruler is straight, and use the craft knife to slowly cut through the beeswax. Apply a firm downward pressure to make sure the wax is cut through completely. Avoid hacking or tearing at the wax. Sharpen the blade or switch knives if necessary.

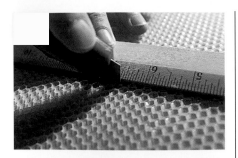

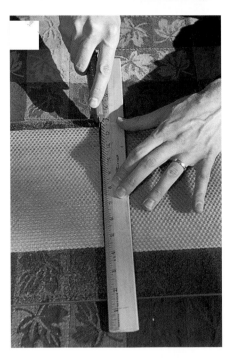

9. Pull the two halves apart.

10. Set one of them aside for later use and place the other on the cutting board.

11. Take a piece of flat-braid wick and place it about $^1/_4$ inch inside the front edge of the sheet.

12. Make sure about 1 inch of wick sticks over the right edge of the sheet. This will be the top of the candle when it is finished.

13. Note that the length of the wick at the bottom of the candle does not matter, for now. It will be trimmed later.

14. Tear away a small hunk of wax from the lower left corner of the sheet. This will be used to prime the wick for burning.

15. The tear in the wax will be hidden from view once the candle is rolled.

16. Press the beeswax into a long, narrow piece. It will become warm from the heat of your hands.

17. Place the piece onto the 1-inch-long section of wick.

18. Press and massage the piece so that it wraps around and covers the wick, allowing the wax to act as fuel for the wick.

19. Make sure the wick stays straight and parallel to the bottom.

20. Starting on the bottom left edge, fold the beeswax over onto the wick. Press down firmly on the wax. The idea is to crimp the wax so the wick is held in place.

21. Slowly move to the right, folding the wax over and pressing it down along the entire length of the edge.

22. If the sheet feels too stiff and is difficult to fold, heat it with a hair dryer for several seconds using a quick side-to-side motion.

23. Once the edge is folded down, it's time to begin rolling.

24. Grip the folded edge and roll it forward gently on itself, making sure the roll stays even.

25. Use the fingertips to press forward evenly along the folded edge. Once one roll with the beeswax has been accomplished, the remainder of the project is easy.

26. Slowly and evenly roll the sheet forward. Be careful not to press down too hard, or the candle might be crushed.

27. Make sure the edge of the rolled, main body of the candle remains even with the edge of the flat section of beeswax.

28. Continue rolling until only the edge of the sheet remains.

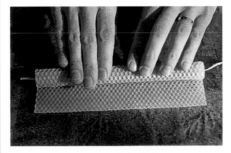

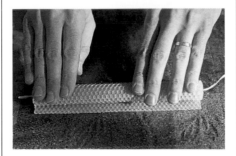

If the roll ever becomes crooked or uneven, simply unroll a small section of the beeswax sheet and try to roll it again.

29. Firmly press this edge flat onto the candle, so that the seam is reduced.

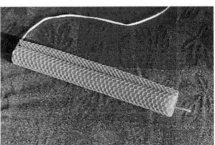

30. Use the hair dryer, if needed, to keep the wax soft and pliable.

31. Trim the wick at the bottom of the candle as flush as possible.

32. The candle is ready to be lit.

TIP

- **Gift shops and candle stores** are littered with the crushed forms of countless beeswax candles handled by curious shoppers. These candles are fragile and are very easily damaged. Handle finished candles with care.

These are based on skills learned in the beeswax candle project.

Rolled spiral beeswax candle

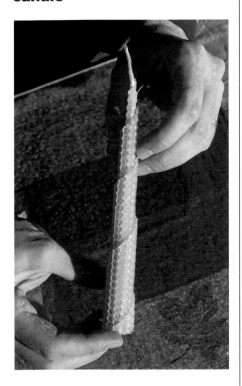

Take half a sheet of beeswax and cut it in half again, diagonally.

Use one of the pieces and line up a section of wick about ¹/₄ inch in from the bottom edge of the sheet. Make sure the wick protrudes about 1 inch over the right edge.

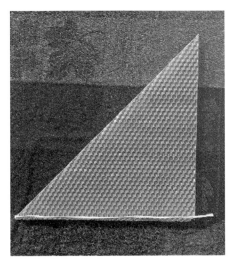

Tear a hunk of wax from the bottom right corner of the sheet.

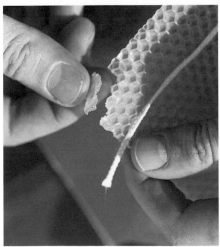

Warm it with the fingers and form it into a thin, narrow piece.

Press the wax onto and around the wick.

Make sure the wick is straight. Fold the bottom edge over the wick, and press down to crimp the wax over the wick.

Roll firmly and evenly with the fingertips until the sheet has been used up. The spiral shape of the candle will become obvious as the rolling progresses.

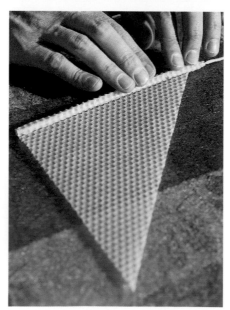

Trim the wick, if necessary.

Two-tone beeswax spiral

Follow the directions detailed above, except use two different colored sheets cut diagonally lengthwise.

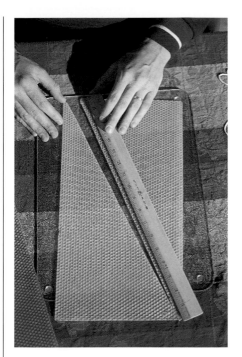

Make sure the edges of the two sheets overlap slightly and are lined up straight.

Roll firmly and evenly with the fingertips until the sheets have been used up.

Trim the wick if necessary.

Resources

BOOKS ABOUT CANDLE MAKING

The following titles contain information, projects, and ideas useful to beginners looking to advance their skills.

Constable, David. *Candlemaking: Creative Designs and Techniques.* Tunbridge Wells, Kent, UK: Search Press, 1992.

Jenkins, Alison. *The Handmade Candle.* Pownal, VT: Storey Books, 2001.

Nichol, Gloria. *Candles: Illuminating Ideas for Creative Candle-Making and Enchanting Displays.* New York: Anness Publishing, 1999.

Oates, Letty. *Naturally Creative Candles.* Iola, WI: Krause Publications, 1997.

Spear, Sue. *Candle Making in a Weekend: Inspirational Ideas and Practical Projects.* Cincinnati: North Light Books, 1999.

RESOURCES ON THE INTERNET

www.candles.org
Website of the National Candle Association. Useful information.

www.candlemaking.org.uk
Website known as the Essential Survival Guide to Candlemaking.

www.candlecauldron.com
Loaded with ideas and tips.

www.thescentreview.com
Good look at the scents available for candle making.

groups.yahoo.com/group/candlemakingsurvival
Online group with thousands of members who exchange ideas and techniques for candle making, from beginner to expert.

Measurement Conversions

Liquid/Dry (U.S.)				Metric
1 teaspoon	=	$^1/_3$ tablespoon	=	5 milliliters (ml)
1 tablespoon	=	3 teaspoons	=	15 ml
$^1/_4$ cup	=	4 tablespoons	=	60 ml
$^1/_2$ cup	=	8 tablespoons	=	118 ml
1 cup	=	16 tablespoons	=	237 ml
1 cup	=	$^1/_2$ pint	=	237 ml
2 cups	=	1 pint	=	473 ml
4 ounces	=	$^1/_2$ cup	=	118 ml
8 ounces	=	1 cup	=	237 ml
16 ounces	=	1 pint / 1 pound	=	473 ml / .45 kilogram / 453 grams
1 quart	=	2 pints	=	946 ml / .95 liter
1 gallon	=	4 quarts	=	3.8 liters